suddenly we

also by evie shockley

POETRY

The Gorgon Goddess

a half-red sea

*31 words * prose poems*

the new black

semiautomatic

CRITICISM

Renegade Poetics: Black Aesthetics and

Formal Innovation in African American Poetry

WESLEYAN POETRY

suddenly

EVIE SHOCKLEY

Wesleyan University Press / Middletown, Connecticut

Wesleyan University Press
Middletown CT 06459
www.wesleyan.edu/wespress

Art © 2012 Willie Cole, courtesy of the artist and
Highpoint Center for Printmaking, Minneapolis

Designed and composed in Adobe Caslon Pro by Mindy Basinger Hill

Library of Congress Cataloging-in-Publication Data

Names: Shockley, Evie, 1965– author.

Title: Suddenly we / Evie Shockley.

Description: First edition. | Middletown, Connecticut : Wesleyan University Press,
[2023] | Series: Wesleyan poetry | Summary: "Shockley repurposes literary and musical
modes from across centuries of African American and diasporic traditions.
Given the choice between formal flawlessness and page-spanning sprawls,
between autobiographical revelation and collective outcry, she welcomes the self-
contradictions of being all the above." — Provided by publisher.

Identifiers: LCCN 2022053758 (print) | LCCN 2022053759 (ebook) |
ISBN 9780819500236 (cloth) | ISBN 9780819500458 (paper) | ISBN 9780819500465 (e-book)

Subjects: BISAC: POETRY / American / African American
& Black | POETRY / Women Authors

Classification: LCC PS3619.H63 S84 2023 (print) |
LCC PS3619.H63 (ebook) | DDC 811/.6—dc23

LC record available at https://lccn.loc.gov/2022053758

LC ebook record available at https://lccn.loc.gov/2022053759

5 4 3 2

for cheryl a. wall

(october 29, 1948 – april 4, 2020)

mentor & friend

professor of black feminist truth & beauty

we should believe,
believe in each other's dreams . . .

—*aretha franklin*

to put it in tweetable terms,
they believed they had to hate black women
in order to be themselves.

—*alexis pauline gumbs*

such the rigors
of

seeming defeat again, the weight we put on
seeming, absecuh's melodic slap. such were
the rigors, made-up words made off with us,
the

we we'd otherwise not be.

—*nathaniel mackey*

there is nowhere you can go and only be with people
who are like you. it's over. give it up.

—*bernice johnson reagon*

contents

suddenly we

alma's arkestral vision (or, farther out)

I.

```
you                     you                 you you
  you                     you           you           you
  you          you        you          you               you
   you      you  you      you       you you you you you me
   you      you   you     you       you
   you   you     you   you          you
    you you      you you              you             you
      you          you                  you you you
```

II.

blue snowflakes

the night falling
through the night

III.

naut	not	knot
knot	naut	not
not	knot	naut
naut	knot	not
not	naut	knot
knot	not	naut

IV.

ship shape
prowless prowl
tail trailing

or have i mist
                ache
                    in
your stern look
for a backwards glance

your blood aboveboard
you're lighter
        on the bottom

v.

thestarsarewh
atshinesinthe
spacesmadeb
etweenuswhe
nwegetcloser

VI.

we sail the starry night
        our brush with the infinite
        our hope-soaked oars stroke
these glittering blues

        we row
        will row
        will have rhone

we wheel on
        un-
        en-
           compassed
look at our space-van go

VII.

against the watery expanse
       our bit of sun raffia
       our bit of sun rapture
       our bit of sun rajah
       our bit of sun radical
       our bit of sun rasta
       our bit of sun random
       our bit of sun ramadan
       our bit of sun ravenous
       our bit of sun raconteur
       our bit of sun razzmatazz

an astral-ark plotting movement
       a course   of action

VIII.

we are the sailors
we are the ship
we are the stars
we are the night

you   can't tell   us (a)   part

IX.

she sees us
    each streak of color

we	*we* nique	
we	*we*	
we	*we*	
we	*we*	in the
we	*we*	
we	*we*	
we	*we* niverse	
	we we we	

—*after alma thomas's* starry night
  and the astronauts *(1972)*

we ::

becoming & going

perched

i am black, comely,
a girl on the cusp of desire.
my dangling toes take the rest
the rest of my body refuses. spine upright,
my pose proposes anticipation. i poise
in copper-colored tension, intent on
manifesting my soul in the discouraging world.

under the rough eyes of others, i stiffen.

if i must be hard, it will be as a tree, alive
with change. inside me, a love of beauty rises
like sap, sprouts from my scalp
and stretches forth. i send out my song, an aria
blue and feathered, and grow toward it,
choirs bare, but soon to bud. i am
black and becoming.

—after alison saar's blue bird

no car for colored [+] ladies
(or, miss wells goes off [on] the rails)

    —memphis, 1883

she wasn't born a hero, you know. once, she
was twenty: four years an orphan, eighteen years

free. with a passion for brontë & a weakness for
fashion, she might drop a month of her schoolteacher's
salary on clothing at menken's palatial emporium,

to dress as befits a lady. she pays to ride first class
that autumn afternoon, knowing she looks the part: full

skirt, cinched waist, gloves, crown. boarding, she peeps
the drunken white man smoking up the "colored car,"

& no. she's not buying it. her place is in the *ladies'* car.
i know she wasn't born a hero, but once ida b. wells

addresses what befits a lady who pays to ride first class
(*to drift into anywhich seat she selects*), she's becoming one.
outfit be damned, she resists her ouster, till her sleeve's

torn & the conductor's bleeding. she'll pull these threads
until the whole *threadbare lie* of lynching unravels.

    —with gratitude to paula giddings

the blessings

the things that i give birth to matter.
the things that i give birth to give birth to other things.
—nikky finney

i gave mine away—
not all, but the greater portion,
some would say. i gave
away the ready claim
to goodness, to purpose. i gave
away mary, sarai,
and isis. i gave away
necessity and invention.
i gave away a whole
holiday, but i kept billie.
i gave away the chance to try
and fail to have it all. i gave
away the one thing
that makes some men
pay. i gave away the pedestal,
the bouquet. i gave away
nel wright, but i kept sula
peace. i gave away
the fine-tooth comb, but
kept the oyster knife. i gave
away the first word
the new mouth forms, the easiest
to parlay across so many
languages. escaping
the maw, i gave away
the power to hold—and be held
in—sway, but i kept
cho, parton, finney, chapman,
and tomei. i gave away the eve
who left the garden

that day, but kept the cool,
green, shady, fruitless,
fruitful stay, the evening
that did not fall
away.

the beauties: third dimension

—after willie cole

LULA BELL

      i'm not the first to feel that tingling
in my fingers, that pull to read the braille
of your body, but i may be the first
        to ask permission. merely to eyeball

      your brocade is to begin weaving a tale,
        a tapestry of travels and chains, joints
and partings. you are stitched with
the trajectories of insects: busy, purposeful,
        multiplicitous. ink-kissed, you cast quite

      an impression. i swallow and desire
tastes of blueberries. i walk away
empty-handed, but heady, carrying
        an eyeful of your texture of caress.

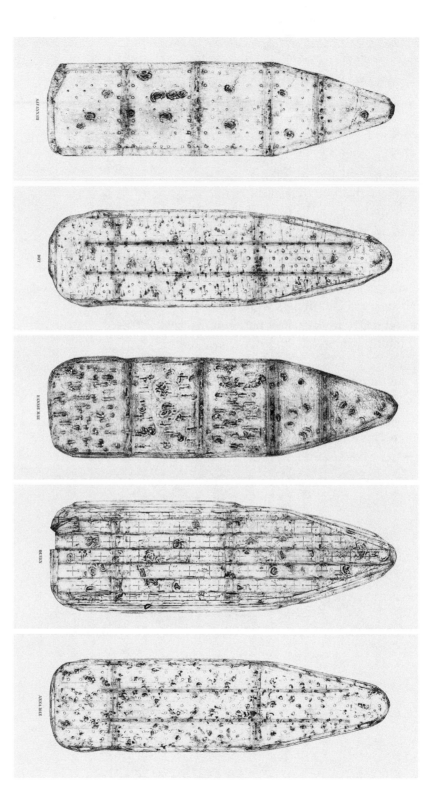

CAROLINA

i'm dark, except where i'm
darker. is that what draws
your eyes to my curves,
the sway in my stance, the still

moving in my stillness? dream
into me: dragonflies, fireworks,
dandelions, and dance. mountains,

doves, caravans, and mosques.
centerstage, a storm of sun
at the edge of a forest, pines
rising past possibility. you

wonder if you could bear all
that life has imprinted upon me.
well, no. but resilience may

be your inheritance, too. it's
just that i make it look good,
softened and rounded by what
leaves so many flat. i stack

up against the intense hostility,
i shroud myself in down
to make my mood light, i show

you the substance of shadow,
let you see what you think
you're seeing through. ink
my reflect-i on white paper.

DOT

you stand, on the stand, evidence
        pedestaled, representing damage
and delight, sun-struck, wind-

            whipped, riddled with the comforts
                    and costs of home. you show me
            what staying gets you. read flatly,

you're the map of being pulled
        in two directions at once. your
third dimension is living *through*.

SAVANNAH

south of somewhere, dry
      or swampy, you are defined

by, thrive on, heat. or you
      steer through water while water

seeps through you. carry
      your bridges where you go,

like the troubled drink they
      span. the damage someone

planned for you is sharp,
      predictable, dull. the darkness

you chose and courted rides
      your skirt up your thigh. you've

planted a foot on the fence
      rail, part stabilizer, part

launching pad. desire blooms
      about your torso like bites

coaxed open with gnawed-off
      nails, like charcoal roses.

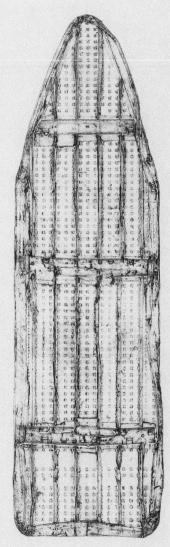

MATTI LEE

MATTI LEE

time for me to make tracks. six lines
running south to north. three stops
along the way i want to leap in passing.

i'm leaving the foothills, low rise
in the earth just high enough to let me

see the first leg of the journey. i'll
have my skirts tucked under me,

stiff as metal, an armor of poplin
and starch. no man will be surprised
to find how much give i have in me,

cuz what i'm giving from above my
hem ain't for him—or him—or him.

see the creases of my knees? look no
farther unless you want your ruffles

feathered. weathered. show me how
smiles pleat your face. there's a pattern
here—you follow? i left tracks for you,

beauty, and i'll be waiting for you up
where all the lines come down to two.

ROSE

wallflower. overlooked or
looked over, but uncited.
anxieties incited, you dig
neatly filed nails into tender

skin, leave traces of nerves
in haphazard crescents up
and down your arms. you
shedded the daily housecoat,

shapeless sack for your work-
aday body, and laced yourself
into a dress bright and floral,
designed for spinning. but

the jitterbug got the jitters,
willed herself into wallpaper.

FANNIE MAE

another day passed in a haze
          of regret. i reap what i have
sown: poppies and showers.

my face is a study in water-
          colors. i tried again to be open,

but even shot through with
          longing, only my scratches
appear visible. my verdant

valley is counted as vacuum.
          i'd give my right eye to be

caught in somebody's cross-
          hatches, to come alive to them,
briefly, if only as a target.

SARAH

girl, you leave me with a faint
flavor of sunflower, of corn
flour, of rainwater, of clouds.
a faded bouquet, treasure
pressed, dressed in a bible's

parchment leaves. girl, you
are a dim remnant of joy
remembered through a haze
of time, the color of youth
washed and worn and washed

and worn until your rainbows
grayed. maybe the violets
can be reactivated—a scratch-
and-sniff that floats parades
of petals to surface. maybe

the hint of beauty in you is
not an afterimage, but a matter
of taste. girl, tell me: have
you lost your spice? stick
out your tongue and say *nah!*

ZEDDIE

backbone. headstrong. arms akimbo,
flaunting your bruises, you wear
your scars like armor. if your look is
penetrating, you're just giving as good

as you get. if we can't imagine what made
you this way, hard-edged and iron-willed,
straightforward and cross, perhaps you're
right to aim at seeming opaque. even so,

you're almost sheer, a linen blind
before a closed window, glassy, paned.

MAMMY

someone turned my strong into wrong,
        my upright into pack mule. i've washed
for whites until my hands're red and my
        spirit nearly (b)leached from my body. i've

served as a container for others' woe.
        someone's been riding my back so long
there're permanent tracks. but pain has
        polished my edges, sharpened my memory.

i haven't always been seen as a smudge.
        i wasn't made for flattening. someone—
someone *else*—knows where to find my
        hidden rivers. another dear someone says

my name so it sounds right, cherished,
        a jewel on the lips of a mouth like mine.

QUEEN

statuesque, enrobed, you command
      attention. hood and cape do not hide,
but frame your glory. are those stars
      inside its folds? are those crosses

wholly imagined? i don't believe my
      eyes have been taught to see your
blossoms as blemishes, your flowers
      as flaws. hold out your arm. embrace
me, drape me in shadows of fabric

aglow with grace i've learned only
      now to interpret. adding abundance.
signs of identity, fluidity. majesty,
      drown me in your midnight reign.

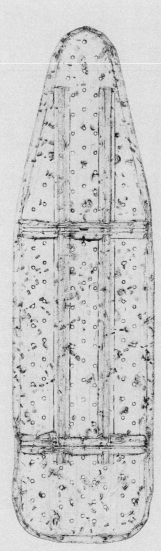

LULA BELL

blues-elegy for cheryl

cheryl wore her hair in a close-braided crown
yes, she kept her hair braided in an elegant crown
hope she was braid-bedecked when they laid her down

she was a preacher's daughter, a queen from queens
raised by devout parents to be a queen from queens
and you could tell by her spine she knew what regal means

now, she was one of the earliest to stake out our field
cheryl was among the early ones cultivating our field
spent years sowing seeds of study—& got to see them yield

she weeded our mothers' gardens with tender loving care
tended hurston & cade & morrison (&&&!) all with loving care
our daughters won't have to search hard for the bounty there

if you wanted to see her glow, call her daughter's name
o, she beamed brightest at the sound of her daughter's name
mothered many literary lights, but camara was her flame

spin a song of respect & let it slide into a blues
raise her a praisesong of respect with a b-side of blues
i got a tall hole full of empty, one that i'll never lose

crystal laughter, diamond smile
wind-chime laughter, sunshine smile
when she laid 'em on you, you could fly awhile

none of us could believe that cheryl's time had come
we were no ways ready to hear her time had come
but she was a natural woman, & nature took her home

—in loving memory of dr. cheryl a. wall

(in)site unseen

grief blows through
     the body ~ a cold wind
          after rain. neither a season
       nor a respecter of seasons ~

shakes chilly drops
     from the heart's greenest
          leaves and barest branches.
       makes the brain its unwilling

pupil, teaching where
     our hollows lie ~ the small
          depressions in which spills
       collect ~ the caverns heaving

with dark. grief plays
     the holes in the ragged, rigid
          soul ~ ruthlessly issuing
       a bone-thin tune locked

in a raw blue key.

sol(ace) song

your laugh is a country road, open,
    made of gravel and shade,
much traveled, before this dark day.

    few things we sojourners
have shaped contain so much space—
    arenas shrink beside its vast

invitation—yet remain spilling full.
    after the passing through
of one too many ones tuned to their

    own inward music, unable
to detect the sound of sun drifting
    or driving down through

oak, willow, and sycamore—not on
    that bright frequency—you
(anyone might) start seeing shadow

    as rain. that water is pain,
but is not the end of your road. listen
    to yourself with the ears

of your sisters, who hear you shining,
    who know right well how
a dense green may seem nearly night.

—for l.

the lost track of time

now that i'm on this track, i can't find my way back
to the main drag. in the middle of 2020, i carelessly
drifted off onto a street not quite a cul-de-sac, but
still sacked or socked in, a cloud having swung so
low i got stuck, the flow of traffic—distinguishable
thursdays, next weeks, augusts, and aughts—
carrying on getting carried away without me, just
~~off-scream~~ off-screen. obscene that i seem to have
delegated dailiness so long that my mind's
convinced it's no longer essential. with last year
misty, my brain has relegated the whole of pre-
pandemic life to a fog. or is that exhaust fumes? will
i need eye surgery to see my way clear back to that
spring in paris, that year in the berkshires, that
north carolina decade? cataracts over cackalack. the
question is: who was i when we last hugged so
close our bones met? where are the coffee spoons of
yesteryear? i've measured out my life in package
deliveries and what's in bloom. the time is now
thirteen boxes past peonies. if you can locate my
whenabouts on a calendar, come get me. i don't
know where i'm going, but i need a ride.

we ::

uppity & down

women's voting rights at one hundred (but who's counting?)

eenie meenie minie moe
catch a voter by her toe
if she hollers then you know
got yourself a real jane crow

~ ~ ~

one vote is an opinion
with a quiet legal force ::
a barely audible beep
in the local traffic, & just
a plashless drop of mercury
in the national thermometer.
but a collectivity of votes
/a flock of votes, a pride of votes,
a murder of votes/ can really
make some noise.

~ ~ ~

one vote begets another
if you make a habit of it.
my mother started taking me
to the polls with her when i
was seven :: small, thrilled
to step in the booth, pull
the drab curtain hush-shut
behind us, & flip the levers
beside each name she pointed
to, the *X*s clicking into view.
there, she called the shots.

~ ~ ~

rich gal, poor gal
hired girl, thief
teacher, journalist
vote your grief

~ ~ ~

one vote's as good as another
:: still, in 1913, illinois's gentle
suffragists, hearing southern
women would resent spotting
mrs. ida b. wells-barnett amidst
white marchers, gently kicked
their sister to the curb. but when
the march kicked off, ida got
right into formation, as planned.
the *tribune*'s photo showed
her present & accounted for.

~ ~ ~

one vote can be hard to keep
an eye on :: but several / *a*
colony of votes / can't scuttle
away unnoticed so easily. my
mother, veteran registrar for
our majority black election
district, once found—after
much searching—two bags
of ballots / *a litter of votes* /
stuffed in a janitorial closet.

~ ~ ~

one-mississippi
two-mississippis

~ ~ ~

one vote was all fannie lou
hamer wanted. in 1962, when
her constitutional right was
over forty years old, she tried
to register. all she got for her
trouble was literacy tested, poll
taxed, fired, evicted, & shot
at. a year of grassroots activism
nearly planted her mississippi
freedom democratic party
in the national convention.

~ ~ ~

one vote per eligible voter
was all stacey abrams needed.
she nearly won the georgia
governor's race in 2018 :: lost by
50,000 / *an unkindness of votes* /
to the man whose job was ~~purg~~
maintaining the voter rolls.
days later, she rolled out plans
for getting voters a fair fight.
it's been two years—& counting.

nature studies

      first, it was a short piece of lupine,
passed around the group, for us
      to smell its intoxicating wine. then,
the toxic corn lily, from which he
      peeled leaf after leaf until nothing
remained, to reveal the illusion
      of stalk. next, a still-berryless sprig
of mistletoe, plucked from the jolly
      parasitic kiss it had given a baby
jeffrey pine's twiggy trunk. &. &.
      my heart snapped with each stem,
every time he stepped off the trail
      to return with a mystery in hand,
a present conjugated into past tense.

fruitful

you grow my garden. no, you are
          the whole of it: the beds of zinnias,
      tiger lilies, begonias, petunias, in all
            their taken-for-granted variety :: irises

waving purple flags from the tops
          of long stalks :: daffodils and violets by
      the bushel, rhododendrons and azaleas
            by the bush. you are the greenhouse

in the western quadrant, the rainforest
          inside, and the delicate herd of orchids,
      strange by stranger, each out-thriving
            the other. not just lovely, you're

the courtyard, central, complete
          with benches for contemplating
      the round, still pool, an eye gazing
            back at the ones looking down. you're

the meadow of tall grasses that hide
          everything but the sound of the stream ::
      the arched boughs of the peach orchard,
            the rows of beans, corn, greens, gourds,

the root vegetables, the parsley, sage,
          rosemary, and chives, oregano, basil,
      and, yes, all the thyme in the world.
            you're the stand of aspens waving me

on :: the grove of willows that arc
          and cascade, but never weep :: the oaks,
      maples, and birches encircling the verge.
            here, i become my best self, i exist at

peace with birds and bees, no knowledge
                    is denied me: i eat the apple, speak
            with the snake, and nothing as obnoxious
                        as an angel could oust me from this soil,

the plot where the best of my stories
                    has its genesis, and finds its end.

dive in

the body, bodies, in a pool of bedding, blue,
            a sea of sweat, shared ~ we each slip into some-

     one more comfortable than loneliness, than
              shame, not easy but something to do with our

        hands, our mouths, till we can forget, let go ~
     yet the body remembers when it was twenty-

something, thirty-something, happy to be
        stroking, stroked, swimming, limbs pulling,

             thrashing, toward the o of oblivion ~ these
      positions still take the body reaching, fluttering,

  grasping, gasping, back to that timeless place, all
    of it happening in the now, in the mind, a transit

           between mind and (__)it, transport, transferring
a rage of pleasure between us ~ the outrageous

       sound of this joy, the silence at center, we're
         in over our heads ~ a body can get carried

    away in that headiness, i did, and you with me,
       swept up in a wave of language and tumbled

what does it mean to be human?

ashes ~ strong sunlight interacting with green, the leaf an engine trembling
in the wind ~ fur and flies ~ the stars behind the clouds ~ gas as a mass ~ the
sweat on my back, carrying down my spine the traces of sweat four centuries
old that ran into wounds ~ recycled survival ~ the blue-black of the pacific
floor and the tentacles pulling life across it ~ the pulsing limitations of a
colossal, spherical home we did not build and will not save ~ tempests ~
the knobs of a sycamore

the perception of these mysteries ~ in the name
of *wonder ~ longing ~ fear ~ love ~ pain*
something vast we seek to squeeze into a small box
     what does it mean to be *human*? ~ why do we care?
special, special animal ~ *human* is a box
500 years old ~ made by men who'd seen the light
reflected off sun-collecting skin, and cowered
     we want in ~ want inside that dark box
     not because it is freeing ~ because *it* sits so high
peering out from the darkness of *human*
they have a panoramic view ~ can see everything
except the earthbound, standing ~ towering
beneath, holding *it* towards our star ~ and shining
     see? ~ they couldn't ~ what being in light meant

in this light

a canvas contains wrung gray clouds

      and the river wrong around tree trunks,

tall and bare to above the waist, crowned

         in dull gold and hazel, nothing to lighten

      our load, our eyeful. || a greener green grows

         as a lettuce row, and a tone arises hinting

rose—the hue of the blue, the kissed color

      of the stucco hulls of houses up the hill,

the dry grass and bark, brown but slightly

         glowing—and a garden opens a canvas

      onto a fairytale. || a road runs down a river,

         lined on the left with trees alive in leaves,

while ancient stone buildings with water

      views stream along right to the right, part

of the canvas in shade and part in june

         sun flame. || a painter provides a season,

      a setting, and an oil-thick frame of mind.

—*after monet's* flood at argenteuil || *pissarro's* vegetable
   garden at the jardin de maubuisson, pontoise || *and sisley's*
   saint-mammès and the slopes of la celle—june morning

"the musician stands out" (or, le musée de l'orangerie *curates a history lesson*)

in the third-to-last room you visit it hung, he was hung, he was hung up, it's a hang-up, you are hung up on this painting, *le noir à la mandoline*, always with, with it, he's with it, the banjo, no, mandolin, the *man* is in the instrument, the black is in the player, the white is in the strings, that's the catch, the song that catches no one by surprise, that catches in his throat, that catches up with him wherever he goes, his eyes round, as black as the hole in his instrument's belly, his arm as brown as the instrument, the *noir* is brown, his lips withhold their hole, the player's (w)hole or (k)not, the hole deepens the song, the instrument has a neck, the player has a tool, it's his hang-up, he's hung up on the tool of his trade, he's hung, it's the trade-off, you're onto it: without it he'd probably be off the wall.

—after andré derain

breonna taylor's final rest
(or, the furies are still activists)

maybe it's your worst nightmare :: a thundering knock
on the door—or no knock, just the lightning-crack

of wood giving way against its nature. maybe you've
never dreamed of such force being used against
you. in your home. in your bed. you are cocooned,

your heartbeat slow. the darkness is part of what
makes you feel safe :: the rest is cotton and flesh—

your lover's—and the peace you've earned tracking
folks' emergencies, back and forth, all damn day. you

remove your uniform, expect to sleep well. instead,
baby, it's your worst nightmare. the thundering knock

of your heart, beating slower. darkness. is part of what
makes us so furious the fact that the same bloody
forces that blue your   life to shreds are still free

to deliver their next bouquet of violents? breonna, rest
assured, tisiphone will help us hunt your justice down.

color bleeding

one year, i carried the blues around
like a baby. sure, my coffee mugs cupped

amethysts :: water gushed, rose-tinted
and -scented, from the faucets at my touch ::
the air orange with butterflies that never

left me. meanwhile, indigo held fast
to my toes :: lapis lapped my fingertips ::

and a hue the shade of mermaid scales
bolted through my hair like lightning.

my eyelids drooped, fell, heavy with sky.
that year i carried the blues around

left me mean :: while indigo held fast,
the daily news tattooed azure to my back.
true, festivals of lilies buoyed me. but what

good could white do? the blues grow like
shadows in late sun :: stretch   creep   run.

destin(ed)ation

i became a fugitive the first
  time i sent the *w* of my wish
    flying into the dandelion's fro

:: that white cloud scattered
  in patterns of maybe and my
    thoughts followed :: maybe

north, maybe france, maybe
  my lips the color i was born
    with :: i became a fugitive

long before i donned the gear,
  by time i slipped myself out
    the box of stockings and heels,

my fugitivity was old hat :: i
  became a fugitive the first time
    i looked around the house

of *could-be-worse* and knew
  a garret could be better, knew
    alone could be better :: long

before i stuffed seeds into
  a pillowcase, packed a bag,
    or earned enough *mad money*

for me to get downright
  fucking furious, i could tell
    i was en route to absent ::

the first time i cast my dreams
  into a future the shape of
    my body, my intellect, my

heart, i was gone :: there was
        no other space that could
                contain me, there was only

the squeeze into obedience's
        shadow and the spill of my
                elsewhere into watchful

silence :: i could act my age,
        behave myself, mind my *p*'s
                and *q*'s, but the leaving was

already going/on :: i became
        a fugitive the first time i
                looked at a wall and saw

a window, when i first felt
        the bloody nubs where my
                wings *already spread* would

                        grow—

migratory patterns: birds of paradise

we ::　flocked west like arrows　　pointing toward　 the elsewhere of
　:　　　:　　unfreedom　　not imagining emptiness　　　not a blank
　:　　　:　　　:　　　:　　canvas　　but maybe　　a map less blanket
　:　　　:　　　:　　　:　　　:　　　:　　　:　　　:　　　　ed　saturate
　:　　　:　　　:　　　:　　　:　　: d　:　　　:　　　with　　grief wi
　:　　　:　　　:　　　:　　　:　　: th　:　　　:　　　　no :: flew
　:　　　:　　　:　　　:　　　:　　: we　:　　　:　　　st　　but not e
　:　　　:　　　　　　　:　　　　　:　　mp　:　　　　　　　　tyhanded
　　　　　:　　　　　　　　:　　　carr　ied　a　　　taste of creole s
　　　　　:　　　　　　　　　　　eas　oning　　un　der our tongue
　　　　　　　　　　　s　a pin　ch of geech　ie in our pocket
　　　　　　　　　　　s and a sh　　eet of atlantic　billow　ing
　　　　　　　　　　　behind u　　s　　like birds of paradise
　　　　　　　　　　　we b　rought our own　　beauty in
　　　　　　　　　　　our　　　　way of doing　　in the s
　　　　　　　　　　　oftn　　ess of a gesture　hand sign
　　　　　　　　　　　aling wel　come and pro　tection
　　　　　　　　w　　　e looke d a　round us　　at this str
　　　　　　　　etch of land in sp　itting distance of the pa
　　　　　　　　cific　where hills roll out into flats so so expo
　　　　　　　　sed to the long evening sun　and thought　we'll
　　　　　　　　make us a world　will plant ourselves　in this subtr
　　　　　　　　opical soil　lay concrete and brick　shelter　spla
　　　　　　　　y white bl　inds against the glare　the gaze　and tuck
　　　　　　　i nto the shadows of　what green we can grow　spiking
　　　　　str　iking　　our rad　ical ideas of　liberation　will always orna
m　ent our li　ves with cheri　shed color and grace　　our windows laced
with　electric ice　everyday　remind us　we　are what we call　home

—*after dannielle bowman's* october's shadows

we ::

indurate & out

virtually free

he can do the running man, but no running. any dance that shows she knows her place. coffle-shuffle merengue or nae-nae. no iron cuffs to chafe the ankle. just jewelry that makes a statement. sends a signal. *you're at the end of a rope. o rope. yr rope.* see marissa stop. stop, marissa, stop. marissa stops and shops for food at the corner store. real groceries are outside her radius. she's got to work within convenience. a perimeter she's made aware of by what she's a-wearing. her reality isn't apparent to the unaided eye. nothing to see here, folks, but surveillance cameras are in place in this place, just in case. catch jamal, tech junkie, hard-wired to his device. tethered by a two-hour battery life to the wall of his history class. jamal got to have that juice. the boy needs an outlet. a.j.'s shackled to a monthly fee for the privilege of parole. their freedom isn't free. these are the people in our neighborhood. on lockdown on the block. it's a negated community. confines virtually invisible, but for the faint red lines.

fire works

—june 19, 2021

they start popping off around
        9:30 p.m., hot sounds, rapid
and loud, in the alley behind

my backyard. juneteenth,
        celebrated for the first time
like this, in my still-blackish

jersey city neighborhood. what's
        the wish that sets these sparks
flying? *happy*? *merry*? last

summer, that alley cracked
        with explosions every evening,
punctuating the day's protests,

reminding us all that patrollers
        still roam the streets in search
of black folks on the loose, ready

to fire a few rounds or make us
        take a knee: whatever works
to keep us in our historically

appointed place. sirens scream,
        and my whole body seizes upon
the idea that someone will go

to jail tonight for being too free
        with their jubilee. joyous june-
teenth to you, as we remember

the release that came to texas
　　　more than two years after two
centuries too late. the struggle

　　　continues—so we get fired up.

can't unsee

the eye is a tool. it takes
available light and makes notes

to self about shape, distance,
mood. the self—brain? mind?

soul?—accumulates and cross-
references these observations

with info from the ear, the skin,
the tongue, turns the memos

into memories we trust to be
true. what looks like wood

will not give beneath our feet.
what sounds like a siren

gives cause for alarm, will
be followed by flashing reds

and blues, or flames, or
a stretcher and a gun. the eye

is the open drawer of a file
cabinet the size of your head,

on the outside, and the size
of your life, on the inside.

what goes in might get
lost, but never goes away.

if beale street could talk, jenkins
says baldwin says, it would say

soft sunshine sweater melting
chocolate. would whisper artist's

inner eye sends notes to hands
about shapes, distances, moods.

would speak on woman spine,
shout about black silence

and eloquent vocal black eyes.
jenkins' *beale street* says see?

the glow fonny's eyes emit
when tish is in view, the ideas

spinning and shifting behind
them when he studies his strange

sculpture-in-progress. see tish
discern that glow through prison

plexiglass, still smoldering through
a gray wash of gray. she can't

unsee the lips she kissed, even
when the mauve is bashed black-

blue—and she can't unsee
the bruise. meanwhile, fonny's

eyes are busily imprinting on his
psyche brutal scenes that befog

her face, that twist and disfigure
the structures he sculpts in his

dreams. his visions always black&
white, even when they're in color.

you can't unkill. and you can't
unjail. the constitution doesn't

yet confer on us the right to not
have to think about this shit. we

thumbs-up a criminal justice system
with cold-blooded murderers in

mind, not the system we'd like
ourselves or our kin to fall into.

have you ever made a mistake?
has a witness ever? an officer?

a jury? a judge? when we think
violent crime, if we see black

skin, history's whispering its old
lies into our colorblind ears,

making it easier for us to say *better
that i'm safe and the criminal's sorry*

than to waste time uttering the word
alleged. you can't unsee slavery.

a woman is innocent until proven
angry. a man is innocent until

he fits the profile. a child is
innocent until she sees her mother

or father in cuffs. can't unsee. set
bail too high and in two weeks

we've upped the odds that a petty
thief becomes a well-connected

felon with even more reasons
to steal. i can't unsee the video

of the school security cop slamming
an african american girl, a student,

to the ground. no, not the north
carolina one, the south carolina

one. no, in texas the girl is latina,
and i can't unsee her abuse either.

      race is a tool. the law is a tool.
      they take power and make

      inhumane order out of human
      chaos. they make floors that will

      not give beneath a brown girl's
      skull. they make officers see black

      and think gun. what sounds
      alarming will be followed by cell

      phone photos and video clips,
      seens that yet another century's

      minds and spirits will file away.

an inoculation against innocence

29 march—20 april, 2020

wwiii floated the globe a common   enemy. as usual, we were all in it

together, *it* being history, *in it* up   to our necks. what good is hand-

washing when the contaminants   coat the surface of everything we

touch: doorknobs, compassion,   healthcare, all teeming with germs

of the past, no less concentrated   for being invisible. we breathe them

as one, in and out, the only kind   of sharing that comes naturally to us.

here, as with the 2nd world war, we   watched it rage overseas at first,

content on the couch of neutrality,   even as it burned through other

peoples' lives—until it seemed   the danger would wash up on

our shores. not realizing we were   already infected, we let history

have its way with us: again, we   clutched our pearls and pointed

the finger of j'accusation east   of eden. *i declare!* we shrieked,

and the war was upon us and in   us, the us of a. we couldn't see

the enemy with the naked eye, but   suddenly we were naked before

the eyes of the world: the empire   worn, no protective clothing, no

tests, no ventilators, no plan. we   were all ready to do the right thing.

but who were *we*, and who were we   to do it *to*? how do you say *god bless you* in asian american? how do you   zoom *remote instruction* across a dark

digital abyss? if the poor folks who   don't get paid sick leave are ringing

up our groceries and delivering   our meals, are we eating our stress

or theirs? what is the value of a   healthy black person on the closed

market? meanwhile, corporations   take another step towards person-

hood, as they reveal that they, too,   are vulnerable to this disease. but

why are they the only ones to get out   on bail? will the folks who can stay

at home pay the ones who can't? will   the hordes hoarding purell remain

70% selfish? and what good is hand-   wringing when the virus looks

like cotton, spreads like dandelions,   and the past's poisonous pesticides

have never been proven effective?   who can provide healthcare while

sick with fear, serving on the front   lines with no magic bullet, not even

a clean pair of gloves? and if war   is *still* the vehicle meant to carry

us out of danger, where the meta-   phorical hell do we think we're

going? last week, a young latino   spoke from the bell of his distress,

his cousin *like a sister* in newark,   newly diagnosed: *so i'm trying*

not to worry, but it's hard to focus   *much on anything else, and i just hope*

something positive will come out   *of all this, we're going to change, right?*

change? change, utterly? what   does history say about our herd immunity to altruism or even   common sense? yet we continue

     to pass around words like *hope*   and *change*, catching terms, contagious

with future, the only other kind of   sharing that comes naturally to us.

one foot out of the panorama

the stress of knowing half a thing

reading the *nytimes* like tea leaves

still cycling through the inside's three settings

cool glow   burning up the wires   somewhere, kansas

it's not a ring light-dress
i'm going out for some sun

breathing the park air with strangers

algae and turtles

the pond in a fountainous mood

wanting you, but
quietly

on the playground   a bunch
of little kids   gathered like psychedelic grapes

beneath a clear bucket   rounded   loosely suspended
within a circle painted orange

slowly filling with water

what language? their high-pitched
chant, chorus courting their fate

i wait to watch it   tip

the many colors—

of swimsuits, of shirts, of skins—
washed   but not away

now hustle   skirt-tail swinging

back to my desk

the rough chair fabrics of summer

askia touré was born with it
lower east side vibe outwilding
tom dent raised blackartsouth in its shade
downtown-boy david henderson
walking the de-eternal streets of harlem
loyd addison's body rhythm erect
in penumbral field

rashida ismaili benin done done that
archie shepp's free
jazz-play paid off
the fun era r y ate ness of n.h. pritchard
ishmael reed, cowboy in the boat with sun ra,
on his way west
lorenzo thomas entering all at
olivar pitcher, man in some lan

ceci   t   (over-shadowed:
          a   brenda w
          y   a
ceci l taylor's agglutinizing bent-time

calvin hernton being   twelve gates at once
                          exit in the world

(over-shadowed:
  brenda w a
          c o t +)

shadow over me
catching rain
catching hell

i stand protected

in relation: a semi-cento with, for,
and about john keene (et al.)

a boy is born. a "negro." an artist.
a boy is born a negro and becomes an artist.
a negro boy is born an artist.
a born artist becomes a negro boy.

he is born to "strivers" in the st. louis bullseye.
    in the storm's eye, amidst riots and vietnam.

he is born to an akan-speaking woman in
    the stables of his father. in colonial massachusetts,
    in what would soon be "revolutionary" times.

he is born in abstraction, emerges from the point
    of his own pen. in graphs, in "anti-kantian" maps,
    "in a field," in "the transverse layer," "the tangential
    layer," "the rupture layer," "the violet layer,"
    and "the compressional layer," all at once.

        he drew compositions, studies, "scenes."
        he invested mental energy into seeing
        what he saw, developing a skill, undertook
        it as a form of education. and they said
        "incapable." they said "traced." they
        said "forged." he put a name to this. in
        a word: "treemonisha," a word that means
        erasure of black talent. a forgotten word of
        salvation from scott joplin's magnificently
        heterogeneous musical lexicon.

                            a relation.

he sang uncontrollably, gold coast lullabies,
christian hymns, irish melodies. he improvised,
and they said *imp*. he counted the beats,
and they said *beating*. he fiddle-dee-dee'd,
and they said "sullen nightingall." they said
"music from a tarpit." they said "to the delight
and horror." he put a name to this. in a word:
"attucks," a word that means freedom is
a condition for which the black body gives blood.

                              a relation.

he spent his days scribbling, penning, drawing
worlds he imagined more habitable than his
own. he devoted his time to this "intimate,"
"determinate act," "the search for an approach
to deconstruct his erasure." and they said
"identity." they said "boundaries." they said
"verisimilitude." he put a name to this. in a word:
"driskell." in a word: "gilliam." in a word: "white."
words that mean geometry following its own
lead, mining its own gaps. words that mean
"connection within disconnection."

                              a relation.

he situates himself, "sublime subject
    of bodily subtraction," "reciting the 'negro'
    poems at one of those gatherings."

he situates himself "in the surrounding woods,"
    "at another safe house run by free blacks."

he situates himself, "an object in field,"
    "at the juncture of numerous conceptual planes."

in memory's halls of funhouse mirrors.
in fiction's reroutings re-righting history.
in poetry's a-lyrical a-linear lines.

being his multiple selves by being with multiplicity.
freeing his aesthetic self to track "ghost paths" he
    creates as others have done and are doing.
seeing the self ("black self"?) in a company.
    accompanied.

                              in relation.

jury duty

almost no one ever goes to trial. nearly all criminal cases [97%]
are resolved through plea bargaining.
—michelle alexander

let us go and make our visit.
—t. s. eliot

no one wants to be there. many of us glitter
      like the sea in sunshine, shedding sweat
or tears at the mere thought of a criminal
      court. such proximity to police, to cuffs
and charges. to be trapped playing a role

in some tragedy, condemner uncomfortably
      close to the condemned. many others think
instantly of opportunity costs: *time is money.*
      who can afford to spend three-to-five days'
worth listening to the lawyers coming and

going through the oceans of files, talking
      of boys who were *no angels*? no. to serve is
a right and our duty, each to each—but
      the potential juror peers into the courtroom
as if it were quarantined for the plague.

                    once years ago, my father served. that evening fell
             stormy, the darkness intensified by winds that made
                our metal screen door buzz like a warped

             harmonica. as we waited dinner for him, the power
               failed. my sister and i, young and younger,
                shrieked till our mom lit the fat candle,

its plastic container painted to look like stained
glass. as we sat distracted by flickering
scenes of jesus's miracles, the phone rang:

our father's one call to tell our mother
the jury would be sequestered overnight—
in courthouse cells, we misbelieved. *daddy's in jail?!*

we girls wailed. our lives had been a steady
caravan of cautions and counsels, inevitably ending
and stay out of prison. we hardly dared

imagine that anyone, once caught behind bars,
emerged again. the next day brought morning sun
and father in the afternoon. we greeted him

as if he'd come from the dead.

would it be a hardship to serve three weeks?, dutiful
jurors in my state are asked. the line to plead

excuses runs long. meanwhile, *money* (or lack
thereof) *is time,* for all the men and women

awaiting trial in cells they can't bail themselves
out of. they hear the prosecutors spooning out

their lives, inviting the accused: *sing to me.* they
sing, a loud chorus of bodies white and brown

and black, flooding prisons in waves, while we
malinger on the beach in our own sequestered

chambers. their human voices wake us, or we drown.

prefixed

—eu-: representing Greek εὐ-, combining form of ἐύς good,
used in neuter form εὖ as adverb = well

will a saeed, felicity, or farah be happy? a name's a tattoo
& maybe a fate. baby, we want to carefully euonym you.

tall & evergreen, fragrant (though flammable, too!)—
relax me, clear me, heal me, you sweet eucalyptus, you.

a desire for the good life—while not inherently taboo—
can be carried far too far. for example, eugenics. eww.

how dare you declare that my statements are untrue!
you'd better speak to me more euphemistically, you!

does a fast, fatal crash appeal? or illness's long adieu?
would you rather linger or have someone euthanize you?

i'll pen an epic on your smiles, sing your virtues on cue,
but—trust me—i'd die if i ever had to eulogize you.

language has *baggage*—but the good news is art can renew
& resee it. i spread the word, poetry's ev(ie)angelist. you?

holla

i don't know what's after
death, but i do know my
ancestors. and if what comes next
wasn't better than *this*
mess, we'd have heard about it. there'd
be some half-embodied, half-
spectral stank attitude
up in the kitchen or on the front
stoop, and wouldn't nobody
get no rest, let alone peace. if what
comes next didn't outstrip
this world for beauty, there'd be
some gangster grievances
to deal with. you think not
harriet tubman nor tupac shakur
would have something to say?
you figure neither ella fitzgerald
nor ella baker would sound
off? do you really believe
that malcolm wouldn't have the means
necessary to let folks know
if he found things unacceptable
at the other end of his transition?
we'd be minding our own business,
and suddenly
a voice carrying 30-odd years of *hell-no*
and 3 continents of *you-gots-to-be-*
kidding-me would be all *SING, MUSE,*
OF THE WRATH OF A PHILLIS, pentameting
all over your i-ams. young emmett
would turn up everywhere we look,
kicked back and whistling *dixie*
from under that cocked fedora
in a very minor key. we'd have ida b. wells
and june jordan reporting

on the universe's dirty drawers, leaving no
question unasked and no record
unread. mlk would give book,
chapter, and verse on the meaning of *promised
land*. du bois would loosen his cravat,
morrison would release her death stare,
and you'd *know* it was on. look,
i don't have the goods
on what comes after death. another pass
at a planet that's still more forest
than concrete? a voyage
into dark matter with a chance
to send our atoms back
as rainfall or baby's breath? a party
hosted on the soular plane
by duke ellington, prince, and ntozake
shange? maybe a front-row seat
for viewing the human animal
finally getting ready to evolve? hey,
someday we'll all get
the dirt. but rest assured, if it wasn't better
than *this* ish, i'd have already gotten
word.

anti-immigration

the black people left, and took with them their furious

      hurricanes and their fire-breathing rap songs melting

the polar ice caps. they left behind the mining jobs,

      but took that nasty black lung disease and the insurance

regulations that loop around everything concerning

      health and care, giant holes of text that all the coverage

falls through. the brown people left, and took with

      them the pesticides collecting like a sheen on the skins

of fruit. they went packing, and packed off with them

      went all the miserable low-paying gigs, the pre-dawn

commutes, the children with expensive special needs

      and the hard-up public schools that tried to meet them.

the brown people left, railroaded into carting off those

      tests that keep your average bright young student outside

the leagues of ivy-lined classrooms, and also hauled off

      their concentrated campuses, their great expectations, their

invasive technology, and the outrageous pay gap between

      a company's c.e.o. and its not-quite-full-time workers. they

took their fragile endangered pandas and species extinction

      and got the hell outta dodge. the black people left and took

hiv/aids, the rest of their plagues, and all that deviant

      sexuality with them. they took their beat-down matriarchies

and endless teen pregnancies, too. those monster-sized

      extended families, the brown people took those. the brown

people boxed up their turbans and suspicious sheet-like

      coverings, their terrifying gun violence, cluster bombs,

and drones, and took the whole bloody mess with them,

      they took war and religious brow-beating tucked under

their robes. they took theocracy and their cruel, unusual

      punishments right back where they came from. finally,

the white people left, as serenely unburdened as when

      they arrived, sailing off from plymouth rock with nothing

in their hands but a recipe for cranberry sauce, a bit

      of corn seed, and the dream of a better life. there were

only certain kinds of people here, after the exodus,

      migrating across the wilderness in search of buffalo,

tobacco, and potable water, determined to discover,

      given all the leave-takings, what they might have left.

ex patria

(fifty days at iliam: shield of achilles)

a mythology begins with a question like *who are we, where are we, what is red, why paint, why me, lord, why?* a person who knows all the answers can only borrow a mythology like *i'm king midas* or *i'm god.* a painter can take a mythology and remake it so that it answers a new question like romare bearden asking odysseus *who are* my *we?* and cy twombly asking akilles *why are we* still *you?* painting the i of the storm on a shield. cutting the trickster out of black and blue paper and lashing him with glue to the mast of his last ship. the journey always rough, some miserable god under land under sea always looking for company, people always succumbing. the hero is the one who comes home, even if it's by process of elimination. a playwright can make a mythology ask *what's wrong with this song?* like suzan-lori parks asking ulysses about coming home from the war *so why are* you *a hero* and *why are you* still *coming home from a war* and *women die in wars too, even if it's not the expected death* and—wait that's not a question but it's still a mythology if that's the only thing she knows for sure.

~ ~ ~

(quattro stagioni: primavera, estate, autunno, inverno)

a mythology can ask *why is autumn so beautiful* and *why is winter, blight-stricken as it is, so arresting?* a mythology, as opposed to a young person, can find autumn and winter much more striking than summer, sun-bleached summer, so legibly the scene of *happiness* that nothing else can really happen there. a mythology can see the blood in spring, the stages of growth a kind of violence the body does to itself, it will never be this way again yet it can't get on to the next moment fast enough. a mythology can ask *why does spring throw its arms out with abandon even when it's abandoning itself?* a mythology can ask *why is winter so much greener than spring, even clouded in white?* the icicles trail as far down the evergreens as they can, but don't keep the wind from brushing snow and sun across the mountain on the same day. the inferno is always burning, women and men going up in flames. a poet can ask *why do daughters grow up by going down?* like rita dove asking persephone *you think* he's *hot?* all the while, autumn is answering the question about gorgeous rotting. just magenta, green, brown, pink, yellow, red, violet flying off the mythological canvas.

~ ~ ~

(untitled [a gathering of time])

a mythology of time can ask a subtle question. a sky blue can gather white clouds right before your eyes holding them by threads of paint stringing us along so that we miss the purple. the thunder is always further away than the whitening. a poet can grab a mythology of time that takes place over the dead bodies of letter after letter. the tongue lays them to rest and they cover are covered by a sheet that falls far from the tree. a cy twombly can leave for rome at twenty-nine and still die an american artist, a hero who doesn't come home. a photographer can snag a mythology to turn her back on it, wearing black and steady gazing from a question that's a statement of the only thing she knows for sure. like carrie mae weems asking institutions like the british museum *when and where i enter* showing that she's the answer. contrast, stark, the steps leading in leading away, bright but heavy. the poet can ask a mythology a question like *what is black in the museums of paris?* and again the mythology pierces the clouds it thunders so loud but so late that by then we've forgotten we saw the lightning we saw the lightning we saw it and it was not subtle.

—at the cy twombly exhibition at centre pompidou, april 2017

we ::

adhere & there

the center of a tension

legislatures in missouri and other states introduce amendments to ban
teaching "an account of u.s. history centered on the implications of slavery."
—abby llorico, ksdk, st. louis, 5/3/21

the earth is a magnificent
complex orb :: a convex womb
of soil whose offspring keep
seeding for siblings :: a conjure
pot of cultures creating
different ways to live
with the gift—joyful, rebellious,
spoiled, attentive ::
a gemstone set in a beautiful
blue bubble, unpopped, bathed
in the warm glow of its own
gold globe. we once taught
ourselves to believe the earth
at the center
of the universe, to see
all the other celestial bodies
encircling it :: the home of god's
most important creation. we
looked and looked
again, using new tools,
sharpened sight. wrenched
from our dream of a starring
role, we learned to despise
learning :: galileo's
unforgiveable offense.

direct to your table

i'll take crab cakes over crab legs because i don't want to work for my food. check, please. here's a tip from the busy waitstaff: we didn't grow it ourselves. farming is an alien concept to most of us. how do you produce the produce? i pop by the corner store looking for slow food. rice? it's a long way from delhi to my local deli. yeah, & this minute maid wasn't made in a minute. some fruit drinks take real concentration. i'd like a slice of cheese product on my ground-up animal. i'd like a spoonful of metabolized corn starch to help my power bar go down. have my food choices been engineered? what's on the label? check, please. check. check. please check.

we'd like to propose—

our daily peaceful multiracial black-lives-interrupted-by-guns-
(& all black lives)-matter protest was interrupted by a gun

our congresswoman's meet-the-people-where-they're-at supermarket
parking lot gab-fest in the southwest was interrupted by a— ✺

our intimate-but-open-hearted-in-mother's-embrace wednesday
evening services prayer request was interrupted by— ✺   ✺

our gatherings in the tree-of-life's-upper-&-lower-branches
observing the holy day of rest, were interrupted— ✺   ✺   ✺

our senior year of high school, warm-mid-winter-in-the-park-
land, o-beautiful-american history test was— ✺   ✺   ✺   ✺

our dorm-life, campus-green, blooming-in-classrooms-where-
poetry-&-engineering-are-professed— ✺   ✺   ✺   ✺   ✺

our weekly hot scene, our night-to-ride-the-latin-pulse, hip-
gripped, zest-sipped, drag-dressed— ✺ ✺ ✺ ✺ ✺ ✺ ✺ ✺ ✺

our calendar—jan. 1st to new year's eve—is shot through, riddled,
with death, every suggested solution interrupted— ✺ (again . . .)

brava gente

where do good people come from?
and how do they come
        to disappear?

floods set us going
famines set us going
fears set us going

we move, propelled by something between drift
        and determination
we migrate, sometimes without hope
        or help

wars explode beneath our feet, so we run
the currents of currency flow from our hands
        to the cities, to the north, to the west,
        so we follow

we flee from destroyed homes to homelessness,
        scatter from exile to exile
our children are born into rupture and unbelonging

the globe is webbed with lines of demarcation
        that trip us as we walk over them,
        that net us as we swim through them

the globe is carpeted with welcome mats
        laid at the back doors, inviting us in
        to cook, clean, sow, harvest, manicure, and build

today's divisions only go back so far
we read the palimpsest of the past
        beneath your tabula rasa, the millennia
        of footsore seekers carrying all the back can bear

all of you were some of us, at one time or another
history holds the long threads that trail from your heels,
        leading back to the origins of your origins

the first fights
the first droughts
the first debts

where do good people rest their heads?
and where will the rest
        of us go?

—for igiaba scego, farah jasmine griffin, dionne brand, suheir hammad,
  cherríe moraga, tina campt, cecilia vicuña, zoë wicomb, layli long
  soldier, min jin lee, and all the many chroniclers of movement(s)

pantoum: 2
                    0
                    2
                    0

who could have predicted this?
          year of unyielding busyness giving way
  to days of utter stillness & bewilderment,
                    streets so quiet they invite coyotes' return.

          year of unyielding busyness giving way
  to dread & longing for another's touch.
                    streets so quiet they invite coyotes' return,
  vehicles parked beneath clearing skies.

dread of & longing for another's touch,
          friendship become a vector for disease.
  vehicles parked beneath clearing skies ::
                    signs of another contagion we carry.

          friendship becomes a vector for disease,
  necessity the mother of transmission.
                    signs of another contagion we carry
  passed around warehouses, factories, plants.

necessity is the mother of transmission.
          some, stuck at home, need soap, puzzles, steaks
  passed through warehouses, factories, plants
                    by others who, essentially, need the work.

          some, stuck home, need toilet paper & tablets.
  year of laboring & learning ever more remotely
                    from others who, essentially, need the work
  that puts them in the virus's line of fire.

year of laboring & learning :: ever more remote
        from the distracting comforts of the old normal.
    what puts some right in the virus's line of fire?
        the viral load like other loads long shouldered.

     without the distracting comforts of the old normal,
it's harder not to see power, raw & rich, shift
        the viral load, like other loads long shouldered,
onto the bodies of black & brown people, the poor.

it's harder not to see power, raw & rich, sifting
     through & into all our media feeds, feeding on us,
on the lives of black & brown people, the poor.
        a march in isolation becomes a summer of marches.

     throughout our news feeds—feeding them & us—
images of injustice emptying or filling our lungs.
        a march of isolation becomes a summer of protests.
    whether from cops or covid, *i can't breathe* ::

evidence of injustice emptying or filling our lungs.
     coronavirus burns through the navajo nation.
    under knees or on ventilators: *i can't breathe.*
        chinatowns excised with breathtaking violence.

     coronavirus burns through new parts of the nation
where mask-wearing's made ideologically toxic.
        anti-immigrant violence :: cutting, breathtakingly
illogical, another symptom of diseased body politic.

with mask-wearing made ideologically toxic
        & medical expertise under increasing attack,
    illogic—one symptom of a diseased body politic—
        struggles with grief for primacy in our days.

     medical expertise warns of variants' attack,
as the numbers of the dead balloon, explode.
        struggles with grief take primacy, our days
    spent coping with curtailed rituals of mourning.

again, the numbers of the dead balloon, explode.
     we go through the motions, familiar & strange,
   try to cope with curtailed rituals of mourning,
       to extend our living through masks & screens.

     we go through the motions, familiar & strange.
year of too many shifts or too little travel,
       of laughing & crying through masks & screens,
   of dystopian fiction & quotidian disaster.

year of unemployment or too stressful travel,
     too much or too little time to contemplate
dystopian depictions of quotidian disaster ::
      what sci-fi & science have been trying to tell us.

     too much to ask that we take time to contemplate
what led us to this paralysis & bewilderment.
      science & sci-fi have been trying to tell us ::
   we could have predicted this. we did.

sonnet for the long second act

your body is still a miracle   thirst
quenched   with water across dry tongue and lips
    or cocoa butter   ashy legs immersed
till shine seen   sheen   the mind too   cups and dips
from its favorite rivers   figures and facts
    slant stories of orbiting   protests or
protons   around daughters or suns :: it backs
up or opens wide to joy's gush   downpour
    the floods the heart pumps   hip hop   doo wop   dub
    veins mining the mud for poetry's *o*
cell after cell drinks   ringgold colors   mulled
    cool cascades of calla lilies :: swallow
and bathe   breathe   believe   through drought you survive
    like the passage schooled you   till rains arrive

—*after alexis pauline gumbs*

facing south

—*after alison saar*

as long as you are south of the canadian border, you are south.
—malcolm x

now, even the north pole is south.
—me

swing low, sweet charioteer, it's the wretched
of the earth you're coming for, who will be found
in the overlooked places. still bent to the soil
and poisoned with it. still chained to each other's
stink and sharing laughter like a virus. still
working through illness and keeling over on
the job. still going hungry to feed the owner's
retirement. still smoothing the sheets the master
poet sleeps on. still torn away from mother,
brother, daughter, lover, earning maybe enough
to keep them clothed, but not to keep them close.

o harriet-chariot, swing lower than maryland,
swing wider. swing by the maquiladoras. swing
by the detention centers. swing by the orange
groves. swing by the slaughterhouses. swing by
the bistros after lunch, the tables heavy on dishes
and light on tips. swing by angola's cotton fields
and compton's streets. swing by the taqueria
and the store-front church. swing by danville, by
oaxaca, by manila. swing by flint. swing by chain
retailers' breakrooms, fast-food restaurants'
kitchens, and every place with *public* in its name.

we see you in harlem, with a dressful of roots
and kin, a look of granite on your face, one hand
open and the other a fist. you're mid-stride
and headed our way. we're coming from deeper,
broader, and further south, at times like you, on
foot, trudging toward a north that's receding
like a glacier. from east and west, we're pushing
towards you, seek citizenship in your determi-
nation. whichever way we're headed, we're
facing the facts. there's no turning back now.

les milles

there is no poem unless   i
we can find the courage to speak

in the middle of a vacation
in the south of france,
a chance to visit a wwii
detention center arises, dusty

and bleak, just outside
aix-en-provence, just past
the scent of lavender, in an

ancient heat. the first thing
you see and the last thing
you visit is a boxcar. you know
what it means. it takes

the same toll on the breath,
the pulse, as the rusted shackles
displayed in another damned

museum. there are histories
of torture preserved all around
us : formally, officially, with
placards and institutional

funding : casually, quietly,
unavoidably, in the quality
of a glance, the poverty of an

existence, the demographics of
a mall, a church, a prison.
in a former tile factory, we learn
again how anything can be

misused, how anyone can be
abused. a kiln is not a dormitory
until it is. here   there   slept

people who were too jewish
to be german, too german
to be french, too despised
and feared to be defended, even

by those who feared they   we
might soon be despised. if i now
say *palestine*, have i forgotten

auschwitz? if i say *settlements*,
have i now forgotten *camps*? if
i don't say *palestine*, have i
forgotten *elmina*, *selma*, *cape town*,

haiti? must every place-name on earth
be a shorthand for violence
on a map of grief?
                    orlando,
            charleston, wounded
        knee, sharpeville, gettysburg,
    tiananmen square, gaza, katyn, plaza
    de mayo, soweto, dominican republic,
        hiroshima, srebrenica, rwanda,
            cambodia, ankara, adana,
                odessa, nanking . . .
                    yesterday

and yesterday's yesterday,
the planet pushing up
sycamores and lavender,
rice and plantains, fertilized

with lead and blood, with rain
from poisonous clouds and
the dust that becomes

of the dead. adam, whose name
means *clay*, was not baked
in a kiln. eve's name means
life, implies the day that follows.

will tomorrow be a place
we can name after something
that grows? what is the proper

use of a wall? there are so many
histories buried in the space
and silence around, within, these
words : these lines make a poor

but portable museum, a set
of sketches—palimpsests, faint
and painfully incomplete—that

map the territory of the human,
with arrows pointing in every
direction : some leading from
you, some leading to you.

                there is no poem unless   you
                we can find the courage to hear.

—*pour les deux milles plus*
  (site-mémorial du camp des milles)

notes

no car for colored [+] ladies (or, miss wells goes off [on] the rails)

This poem would not be possible without historian Paula Giddings's brilliant, evocative, and deeply researched biography, *Ida: A Sword Among Lions: Ida B. Wells and the Campaign Against Lynching.*

the beauties: third dimension

In the spring of 2019, the Radcliffe Institute for Advanced Studies mounted an exhibition of New Jersey artist Willie Cole's stunning print series, *Beauties.* His life-sized prints were made by flattening old ironing boards to the point that they could be inked for printmaking. Cole titled each print with a woman's name, an homage to family members and other Black women from the era when ironing was both drudgery and a skill. The images from the series reproduced in these pages are, in order of appearance: Five Beauties Rising Suite [*Savannah, Dot, Fannie Mae, Queen,* and *Anna Mae*], *Matti Lee,* and *Lula Bell.*

blues-elegy for cheryl

Cheryl A. Wall (1948–2020) was among the scholars who began working in the 1970s and '80s to introduce and institutionalize the African American literary tradition as a field of study within the academy. Her books—including *Women of the Harlem Renaissance, Worrying the Line: Black Women Writers, Lineage, and Literary Tradition,* and *On Freedom and the Will to Adorn: The Art of the African American Essay*—are an education in themselves. She made her transition just three months before she would have retired from Rutgers University, New Brunswick, where she was the Board of Governors Zora Neale Hurston Distinguished Professor of English. She was a consummate scholar and mentor, an enthusiastic patron of the arts, an impassioned devotee of Aretha Franklin, and a dear friend, among many other things. I will never be done missing her.

the lost track of time

I am not T. S. Eliot's Prufrock, but in the moment of this poem, his sense of temporality rang a bell for me.

women's voting rights at one hundred (but who's counting?)

I was delighted to write this poem, at the request of the Academy of American Poets, for the 2020 centenary of the 19th Amendment to the U.S. Constitution. The "two years" reference in the final lines is tied to that date—but those of us who *are* counting can mentally amend that number until Stacey Abrams's organization, Fair Fight, is no longer necessary.

what does it mean to be human?

I am urged to come back to this question again and again by such thinkers as Sonia Sanchez and Sylvia Wynter.

"the musician stands out" (or, *le musée de l'orangerie* curates a history lesson)

In 2017, when I came upon this André Derain painting at the Musée de l'Orangerie, the museum's (English language) website placed the painting in relation to similar images of (racially unmarked) musicians painted by Manet, without comment on the apparent racial difference of Derain's subject. The museum's description of the image provided me with language to play around with as well as my poem's title: "The musician stands out against a plain ochre background animated only by the varying angles of the brushstrokes and a light shadow in the lower right hand section. Derain's freedom of texture and violent contrasts greatly enhance his models. The light on the shirt is expressed by broad areas of white impasto, the shadows by vigorous black brushstrokes. The same contrast is inverted on the neck of the mandolin. Small, delicate touch of white on the face—the eyes, nose and lips—animate the portrait. *The Black Man with Mandolin* is a veritable symphony in brown, ochre and white." Notably, the museum has since retitled the image "Man with Mandolin" ("Le Joueur de mandoline").

can't unsee

Some of the research I did for this poem is particularly worth citing/sharing. First, this article: "Unable to Post Bail? You Will Pay for That for Many Years," by Seema Jayachandran, *New York Times*, March 1, 2019. Additionally, these three news stories, which include video documentation of how violently Black and Latina girls have been treated in their schools: "Video shows North Carolina school officer slamming girl, 15, to floor," by Holly Yan, *CNN*, January 4,

2017; "Video Shows Cop Body Slamming High School Girl in S.C. Classroom," by Tim Stelloh and Tracy Connor, *NBC News*, October 26, 2015; "Texas Officer, Caught on Video Throwing Girl to the Ground, Is Fired," by Christine Hauser, *New York Times*, April 11, 2016. Viewer discretion is advised.

an inoculation against innocence

I was invited to write a poem for an anthology responding to the coronavirus pandemic, just a few weeks into the global reckoning with its transmissibility and lethality. This is the poem I produced, knowing that it would be premature as a reflection upon the significance or consequences of the virus. I include it, unrevised, as a time-stamped snapshot of how the world struck me in that surreal period.

one foot out of the panorama

We all got tired of the word "pandemic," didn't we?

in relation: a semi-cento with, for, and about john keene (et al.)

To create this poem, I juxtaposed moments from John Keene's first three books that seem to articulate parallel concerns. I drew from the autobiographical prose poems of *Annotations*, the short story "An Outtake from the Ideological Origins of the American Revolution" in *Counternarratives*, and the "abstract" poems in *Seismosis* (a collaborative project with artist Christopher Stackhouse), cycling through them in that order. In each of the works—whether writing about himself, the fictional colonial-era character Zion, or Stackhouse, respectively—Keene is careful to situate the black male artist in relation with others.

ex patria

The three sections of this poem take their titles from paintings by Cy Twombly that were on view at the retrospective of his work at Centre Pompidou in the spring of 2017.

brava gente

This piece is informed by a series of articles in *Public Books* on "Black Italy," beginning with a piece written by Giulia Riccò ("Reimagining Italy through Black Women's Eyes"). She discusses Igiaba Scego's historical novel *La Linea del Colore*, now translated by John Cullen and Gregory Conti as *The Color Line* (Other Press, 2022). My gratitude to the brilliant Annette Joseph-Gabriel, who commissioned Riccò's article. I am also leaning on a whole library of thinkers, some of whom I name in the poem's dedication.

sonnet for the long second act

I wrote this piece in conversation with and in appreciation of Alexis Pauline Gumbs's brilliant book of prose poetry, *M Archive*.

acknowledgments

I gratefully acknowledge the editors, publishers, and others thanks to whom these poems have previously appeared (sometimes in different form or format):

"perched," in *Alison Saar: Of Aether and Earthe.*

"no car for colored [+] ladies (or, miss wells goes off [on] the rails)," in *The 1619 Project: A New Origin Story.*

"LULA BELL," "FANNIE MAE," and "SARAH" (from "the beauties: third dimension") and "destin(ed)ation," forthcoming in *Gulf Coast.*

"CAROLINA" (from "the beauties: third dimension") and "in this light," in *Stand.*

"DOT" (from "the beauties: third dimension"), as the text for Marta Gentilucci's *Canzoniere* — Part II, song VII.

"MATTI LEE" (from "the beauties: third dimension") and "facing south," forthcoming in *Feminist Studies.*

"ZEDDIE" (from "the beauties: third dimension"), in *Radiant with Sound,* a limited edition chapbook produced by the 2022 Graduate Letterpress Workshop, Princeton University.

"sol(ace) song," in *Jewish Currents.*

"the lost track of time," "nature studies," and "can't unsee," in *The Kenyon Review.*

"women's voting rights at one hundred (but who's counting?)," in *American Poets,* and subsequently in *underbelly* and *The Best American Poetry 2021.*

"fruitful," in *The Southampton Review.*

"dive in," in *Tin House Online.*

"what does it mean to be human?," in *Ploughshares.*

"'the musician stands out' (or, *le musée de l'orangerie* curates a history lesson)," in *The Spectacle.*

"breonna taylor's final rest (or, the furies are still activists)," in *Good River Review*.

"color bleeding" and "sonnet for the long second act," in the Academy of American Poets' *Poem-a-Day* series.

"migratory patterns: birds of paradise," commissioned by Radius Books for *Three*.

"virtually free," in *Lana Turner: a journal of poetry & opinion*.

"an inoculation against innocence," in *Together in a Sudden Strangeness: America's Poets Respond to the Pandemic*.

"in relation: a semi-cento with, for, and about john keene (et al.)," in *Obsidian*.

"jury duty," in *Sewanee Review*.

"prefixed," in *Written Here + There: The Community of Writers Poetry Review*.

"anti-immigration," in the Poetry Foundation's *Poetry Now* series.

"ex patria," in *The Paris Review*.

"the center of a tension," in *The New Republic*.

"direct to your table," in *Prairie Schooner*.

"we'd like to propose—," in *Adi Magazine*.

"brava gente," as part of the text for *moving still — processional crossings*, a processional opera composed by Marta Gentilucci.

"pantoum: 2020," forthcoming in *Reckonings: A Rutgers Anthology*.

"les milles," in *Boston Review*.

During the period in which most of these poems were written, often either the time or the creative wellspring that I need to write was in short supply. At many points, I only managed to find the energy to produce poems when directly asked to do so. To those who reached out with warm invitations and gentle requests, whether they led to poems or not, I offer gratitude.

I'm deeply indebted to the institutions that provided me with some of that time and space necessary to refilling the well and tuning in to the muse. In particular, I'd like to thank the Radcliffe Institute for Advanced Study (now the Harvard Radcliffe Institute), for an invigorating fellowship (thanks, as well, to my terrific student Research Partner, David Xiang); the Lannan Foundation, for the support and affirmation of the Lannan Literary Award; the University of Arizona Poetry Center, for the Art for Justice commission that pushed me to learn and write more about mass incarceration and towards prison abolition; the English Department at Washington University in St. Louis, for the brief but wonderful residency that comes with the Visiting Hurst Professorship; and Cave Canem, the Community of Writers, Juniper Institute, and Tin House, for generative retreats that invited (or required!) me to write alongside the poets in my workshops. Thanks also to the many people at Rutgers University whose support, flexibility, and encouragement have helped make this book possible.

Among the many artists whose work inspires me, I owe special gratitude to Dannielle Bowman, for inviting me to write a piece in conversation with her subtle and layered photography; to Marta Gentilucci, for inviting me to write poems for her to use in her stunning musical compositions; to Willie Cole, for graciously permitting me to reproduce images from his powerful *Beauties* series in these pages; and to Alison Saar, not only for her genius and moving art (including the piece gracing the cover of this volume), but for an open-ended series of magical collaborations and a cherished friendship.

This book would not be what it is without the unwavering support, insight, encouragement, and vision of the small but mighty team of people at Wesleyan University Press. My thanks to them all—especially Suzanna Tamminen and Stephanie Elliott Prieto, whom I've had the pleasure of working with since I first began publishing with Wesleyan. Additional thanks to Jim Schley for remarkably sharp and sensitive copyediting that really strengthened this volume.

For conversations about poetry and poetics that both expand and sharpen my sense of what's possible and urgent in this art form, I am especially grateful to Tonya Foster, Cathy Park Hong, Douglas Kearney, Ed Roberson, Solmaz Sharif, Phillip Williams, and Javier Zamora. For invaluable, life-saving, Black feminist community at the intersection of activism and poetry, I sing gratitude and love to my sisters in the Poets at the End of the World collective: Ama

Codjoe, Donika Kelly, Nicole Sealey, and Lyrae Van Clief-Stefanon. And for reading drafts of the manuscript that became this book and offering the honest, incisive, generous feedback that equipped me to really *see* what I was doing—and what I still needed to do—in this work, boundless thanks to Claire Schwartz, and—again—Doug and Lyrae.

I'm grateful beyond words to my cherished mother, Leatha Shockley, for her tireless support of and interest in my poetry (and anything else I pursue). She and my whole fam (OH & GA!) buoy me. Finally, for being my trusted first reader, my constant companion through the darkest days of the pandemic, and my dearest and best friend, to Stéphane Robolin: my enduring love.

about the author

Evie Shockley is the author of multiple books of poetry, including *the new black*, which received the 2012 Hurston/Wright Legacy Award in Poetry, and *semiautomatic*, which received the 2018 Hurston/Wright Legacy Award and was a finalist for the LA Times Book Prize and the Pulitzer Prize. Her work has also been honored with the Lannan Literary Award for Poetry, the Holmes National Poetry Prize, and the Stephen Henderson Award. She is the Zora Neale Hurston Distinguished Professor of English at Rutgers University.